Charles Rennie Mackintosh
Hill House

Residential Masterpieces 11
Charles Rennie Mackintosh
Hill House

Text by Yoshio Futagawa
Edited and photographed by Yukio Futagawa
Art direction: Gan Hosoya

Copyright © 2011 A.D.A. EDITA Tokyo Co., Ltd.
3-12-14 Sendagaya, Shibuya-ku, Tokyo 151-0051, Japan
All rights reserved. No part of this publication may be reproduced,
stored in a retrieval system, or transmitted,
in any form or by any means, electronic, mechanical,
photocopying, recording, or otherwise,
without permission in writing from the publisher.

Copyright of photographs © 2011 GA photographers

Printed and bound in Japan

ISBN 978-4-87140-636-9 C1352

Residential Masterpieces 11

Charles Rennie Mackintosh

Hill House

Helensburgh, Scotland, U.K., 1902-04

Text by Yoshio Futagawa

Edited and Photographed by Yukio Futagawa

世界現代住宅全集11
チャールズ・レニー・マッキントッシュ
ヒル・ハウス
イギリス，スコットランド，ヘレンズバラ
1902-04
文：二川由夫
企画・編集・撮影：二川幸夫

GA

ヒル・ハウス——二川由夫
Hill House *by Yoshio Futagawa*

二人の建築家

20世紀初頭，産業革命後の大英帝国に活躍した二人の建築家＝エドウィン・ラッチェンス（1869-1944年）とチャールズ・レニー・マッキントッシュ（1868-1928年）は一つ違いの同世代であった。当時，すでに統合されていた二つの国＝イングランドとスコットランドの間に残る文化的対立関係と相似するかのように現れた二人の建築家は，それぞれの創作のベクトルは違っていたものの，彼らの残した作品は，その後急激に世界中に展開していく近代，そして現代にまで続く建築の進化・変貌を予感させる近代・現代性をすでに持っていた点において，並び評されるべきものである。二人の，卓越した建築手法と類い稀な感性は，単なる伝統・様式の踏襲に留まることなく，新たな発見を伴って近代建築を開く礎となったのである。

20世紀を迎えた英国の建築は，前世紀，ヴィクトリア期にウィリアム・モリスの残したアーツ・アンド・クラフツ運動に根ざした古典様式への回帰の興奮と，中世にまで遡る優雅な芸術への高い関心の中に依然としてあり，この二人の建築家もその例外ではなく，基本的には当時規範とされた様々な伝統的な様式に根ざした設計活動を行なっていた。しかしながら，この二人が共通して他の建築家と全く違う点は，その創作が単なる新古典主義的な模倣と再現の手法ではなく，そこから逸脱していこうとする新しいエネルギーを放っていたことであった。産業革命以降，新たに市民生活にもたらされたテクノロジー，社会構造やそれらに伴う家族関係の変化に，それまでの建築様式は急激に形骸化し，それを頼りにする建築手法が無効化したことをいち早く意識的／無意識的に認知し，新しい手法により，伝統や様式をそれまでとは違うかたちで手がかりとして，新しい建築の地平を目指したのである。

しかしながら，当時の二人の建築に対する評価は対照的なものであった。イングランドのラッチェンスは英国建築の正調なる作家として評価され，対して，スコットランドのマッキントッシュはその逸脱性ゆえに，アーツ・アンド・クラフツ展協会から展示参加を拒否され，代わりにヨーロッパ大陸において多大な支持を得ることとなり，結局，後世においては近代建築を開くイコンとして祭り上げられることとなるのである。

ラッチェンスがアーツ・アンド・クラフツの正調なフォロワーであり，「最後の伝統建築家」ということは長い間，多くの歴史家に認められ，広められていた紛れも無い事実である。さらに，フランク・ロイド・ライトをはじめとする近代建築家がその作品を高く評価し，初期の作品に多くの影響を見いだすことができることからも明らかな様に，その手法とそこに生まれた建築は当時としては類い稀な質をそなえ，近代・現代の建築手法に通じるものであったと言えよう。

ラッチェンスの手法は，建築を，従来のような一様式が定める所作によってつくり出されるものではなく，当時の歴史，文化を横断し，

Two Architects

Edwin Lutyens (1869-1944) and Charles Rennie Mackintosh (1868-1928) are two architects from the post-industrial British Empire of the early 20th century who shared the same generation, their births being a year apart. The emergence of the two architects was analogical with the cultural confrontation that remained between two countries that had already been unified at that time: England and Scotland. Although their creative vectors pointed to different directions, their works call to be discussed side by side in that they were already equipped with Modernity/Contemporarity that was predictive of architecture's subsequent evolution/transformation that developed rapidly throughout the world during the Modern and Contemporary eras. Their remarkable architectural methods and unparalleled sensitivities have set the groundwork for the coming of the Modern architecture through new discoveries rather than limiting themselves to simply following traditions and styles.

Architecture in Britain as it entered the 20th century was still in the midst of the excitement for a return to the Classical style rooted in the Arts and Crafts Movement by William Morris from the Victorian era in the past century, and a high level of interest in an elegant art that traces back to the Middle Ages. The two men were no exception, and performed their design activities based mostly on various traditional styles that were regarded as standard at the time. However, both were totally different from other architects in that their creativity were, instead of being mere neoclassicist methods of imitation and recreation, radiating a new energy that sought to depart from them. Following the Industrial Revolution, earlier architectural styles quickly lost substance along the changes in family relationships, social structures and technologies that were newly brought to public life, and architectural methods that relied on such earlier styles have become invalid. The two architects were among the first to consciously/unconsciously recognize the change, and headed to a new architectural horizon using traditions and styles as clues in a new different manner.

However, appreciation given to each of them at the time was contrasting: Lutyens from England was approved as an orthodox artist of British architecture, while Mackintosh from Scotland was finally rejected joining exhibitions by the Arts and Crafts Exhibition Society due to his deviancy. The latter instead came to acquire heavy support on the European continent, and was eventually mythologized as a pioneering icon of Modern architecture by later generations.

That Lutyens being an orthodox follower of Arts and Crafts and the 'last of the traditional architects' is an indisputable truth that has long been acknowledged and made widely popular by many historians. Furthermore, as it is clear from the fact that Modern architects such as Frank Lloyd Wright acclaimed his work and many traces of his influence can be found in their early works, his methods and architecture had an incomparable quality for that time, one which lead to Modern/Contemporary architectural methods.

His way of collecting elements derived by various different styles and other cultures and refining them in an eclectic man-

様々な異なる様式や他文化からもたらされるエレメントを集積，メタフォリカルな言語操作として折衷的に成立させており，新しい様相，空間に仕立て上げていくその方法は実に現代的である。それは20世紀後半に世界を席巻したポスト・モダニズムの手法を既に実践するものであった。ラッチェンスの設計活動は長く，アーツ・アンド・クラフツの代表的な作家となり，後年には，旧植民地であるインドの首都ニューデリーの都市計画にまで及ぶ国家的建築家にまで登り詰めている。

マッキントッシュはロンドンから遠く離れたグラスゴーの地で，モリスのアーツ・アンド・クラフツの精神を自らのバックグラウンドであるスコットランド文化に当てはめて解釈する。当時，この地に流行していた伝統的なヴァナキュラー建築様式であるバロニアル様式のリヴァイヴァリズムを礎として自らのスタイルを模索していく。

バロニアル様式は，スコットランド固有の民家の建築様式であり，厳しい北の気候，ケルト文化の影響のある力強いバロック様式である。しかし，彼の革新性は，そこに留まることなく，先人の残した様式・マナーをそのまま踏襲するのではなく，一つの手がかり，フレームとして拡大解釈し，工芸的な手法を用い，幾何学的な抽象化を加えたり，東洋，中国や日本を含む他文化からの影響を吸収し，それらを天才的な美的感性によって折衷的に発展・昇華させて新しいクリエイションに仕立て上げていった。「ザ・フォー」と呼ばれるマッキントッシュとその仲間達の活動は，アーツ・アンド・クラフツ運動の精神に則った地点から出発したものであったが，「グラスゴー・スタイル」は後に，その歴史主義から逸脱していく先進性によってアーツ・アンド・クラフツ展協会から拒否されてしまう。

自国での冷遇と対照的に，マッキントッシュの建築は，その洗練された美的世界観が認められ，ヨーロッパ大陸に雑誌や展覧会によって紹介される。当時，ヨーロッパ大陸に起こりつつあったセセッションやアール・ヌーヴォーといった新しい芸術，建築の潮流と交流し，大きな影響を相互に与え合うこととなった。ヨゼフ・ホフマンやヨゼフ・マリア・オルブリッヒらのウィーンの分離派は，その美的世界に自分たちの理念を重ね合わせて称賛し，彼を展覧会に招待することになる。グラスゴーに実現した作品群に見られる繊細で洗練された装飾性は，遠く離れたウィーンのセセッションの目指したところと似ていたが，実はそれぞれが目指す地平は若干違っていた。マッキントッシュは，セセッションやアール・ヌーヴォーからの評価，後年のニコラウス・ペヴスナーの歴史家的な指摘により，近代建築の先駆的建築家というレッテルを貼られるわけだが，自身はその革新性を自覚して「建築家」としてそのスタイルを外に向けて発展させていくような欲を持っていなかったようであり，それぞれの作品は個人的な美的空間への純粋な探求心の結晶に留まっている。残念なことに，ラッチェンスとは対照的にマッキントッシュは後年，建築の仕事に恵まれず，水彩画家としてその生涯を終えている。

ner through manipulation of metaphorical language into a new mode and space is indeed quite contemporary, as it was a precursor of Post-Modernist methods that later dominated the world in the latter half of 20th century. Lutyens' design activity lasted for a long time: he became a leading figure of the Arts and Crafts, and rose to the top in his later years to become a national architect involved in the urban planning of New Delhi, the capital of the former British colony, India.

Meanwhile Mackintosh, in Glasgow far from London, tried to interpret the spirit of Morris' Arts and Crafts by applying it to the Scottish culture that was his own background. He worked to find a style of his own based on the revivalism of the Baronial style, a traditional, vernacular architectural style that was popular back then.

The Baronial style is an architectural style for residential architecture characteristic of Scotland, and consists of a powerful Baroque style influenced by Celtic culture and rigorous northern climate. But his innovation reached further to stretching the legacy of styles and manners as a clue or a framework rather than following it as it is, adding geometrical abstraction using craftwork methods, and absorbing influences from other cultures including Asian, Chinese and Japanese then developing/sublimating them through eclectic approach into a new creation by making use of his aesthetic sensibility of a genius. Although the collective activities of Mackintosh and his fellow artists called "The Four" has originally started by following the spirit of the Arts and Crafts Movement, the 'Glasgow Style' later came to be rejected from the Arts and Crafts Exhibition Society due to its innovativeness that seemed to deviate from historicism.

In contrast with the cold reception given by his home country, Mackintosh's architecture and its sophisticated aesthetic perspective of the world gained acclaim on the European continent and came to be introduced through press and exhibitions. His interaction with new currents of art and architecture such as the Secession and Art Nouveau that were emerging from the European continent resulted in a mutual impact on both sides. Members of the Vienna Secession such as Josef Hofmann and Joseph Maria Olbrich hailed him in admiration as they identified their own ideals with his aesthetic world, and invited him for exhibitions. The subtle, sophisticated decorations found among his works in Glasgow were similar to what the Secession had aimed for far away in Vienna, but in fact their goals proved to be somewhat different from one another. Eventually, appreciation from the Secession and Art Nouveau as well as Nikolaus Pevsner's historical remark in later years came to label Mackintosh as a pioneer architect of Modern architecture, but the architect himself seemed to have lived without being conscious of his own innovative aspect and without a desire to expand his style to the outside world as an 'architect', as each of his works never surpasses the realm of pure, crystallized inquisitive mind for a personal aesthetic world. As opposed to Lutyens, Mackintosh was not fortunate enough to enjoy his architectural practice and ended his life as a watercolor artist.

「ヒル・ハウス」
グラスゴーは産業革命以降，スコットランド最大の工業都市となり，綿工業や造船業を中心に繁栄する。この街から北西へ約35キロ離れた町，ヘレンズバラは，産業革命の恩恵である蒸気機関車による鉄道網によって生まれた新興住宅地であった。ヒル・ハウスの施主，ウォルター・W・ブラッキーはグラスゴーで出版業を営む実業家で，ヘレンズバラの街とその先に広がるクライド川の河口を見渡すことのできる，小高い丘の上の芋畑だった土地を購入し，同郷のマッキントッシュに住宅の設計を依頼することになった。マッキントッシュはここで，建築のみならず，家具，絨毯や照明器具から，壁紙のパターンや暖炉に与えられたインレイなど，この住宅の細部に至るまでのデザインを総合的に成し遂げ，建築家の卓越した美意識を実現している。

住宅の外観はその美しく饒舌な内部空間群に比べて，やや無口なものである。軒の浅いスレート葺きの急勾配の屋根，灰色の荒々しい仕上げの壁とグリッドに割られた小さい窓，シンプルな玄関，飾りの無い煙突群，あまり多くを表現しないこれらのエレメントの構成は，スコットランドの厳しい自然への機能的な対応であるとともにそれ自体を表象するものである。基本的に当時流行したバロニアル様式の精神を踏襲したものであるが，その抽象的なシルエットは後世の近代建築を予感させる斬新なものでもあった。

全体のプランは，家族のための居間，食堂，寝室といった主空間群を収めるメイン・ウイングと，台所や家事室などのユーティリティーを収めるサービス・ウイングが直交したL字型である。これは当時流行していたゴシック・リヴァイヴァルを基本として，当時の新しいライフスタイルに対応した住宅形式であり，たとえば，ペヴスナーが近代住宅建築の起源と位置付けたモリス邸であるフィリップ・ウェッブ設計の「レッド・ハウス」のプランも同様のL字型であった。メイン・ウイングは北側にホール，廊下，その南側に諸室が配された北廊下型で，南側の青芝に覆われた庭とその先に広がる街や河口の風景を諸室に獲得するものである。L字型の角部に置かれたサービスのための螺旋階段は，主従空間の境界となり，外観上の焦点にもなっている。

この規模の住宅にしては小さく取られた玄関は建物西端に位置し，その外観はあまりにも簡素なものであるが，一度内部に導かれると，その印象を拭い去る芳醇な空間連鎖が広がる。玄関から階段室，ホールと続く北側に配置された動線空間に沿って，主人の書斎である図書室，居間，食堂が並ぶ。同様に，2階も北側の廊下，ホールに沿って寝室群が配置されている。これらはそれぞれに異なる趣向のインテリア・デザインが巧みに与えられている。

主要な空間は夫妻に向けた，当時のジェンダーを表象するデザインがなされている。図書室や食堂は主人の空間として男性的な「黒」の空間であり，対照的な居間や2階の主寝室は夫人に捧げられたフェミニンな「白」の空間である。男の空間である図書室や食堂は，木部が

HILL HOUSE
Since the Industrial Revolution, Glasgow has grown into Scotland's largest industrial city as it prospered mainly from cotton and dock industries. Helensburgh, a town approximately 35 kilometers northwest of Glasgow, was a new residential area born as a byproduct of a steam locomotive railway network. The Hill House client Walter W. Blackie was the owner of a publishing house in Glasgow. He has purchased a former potato field on a small hill overlooking the town of Helensburgh and the mouth of Clyde River that stretches beyond, and decided to appoint Mackintosh, a fellow countryman, to design his home. Here, Mackintosh achieved a comprehensive design for not only the building but for every details of the house from the furniture, carpet and luminaire to wallpaper pattern and inlay for the fireplace, materializing the architect's distinguished sense of beauty.

Exterior looks of the house is rather taciturn compared to the attractive, verbose group of interior spaces. Steep slate roof with shallow eaves, roughly finished grey walls with small gridded windows, plain entrance, unadorned chimneys—the composition of such elements that seem to have little to express is a functional response to nature's severity in Scotland as well as a representation of itself. It basically follows the spirit of the Baronial style which was popular back then, yet its abstract silhouette was before the times, as if foreseeing the Modern architecture of later decades.

The overall plan consists of the main wing housing the main spaces such as the family living room, dining room and bedrooms, and the service wing housing the utilities such as the kitchen and housekeeping room, placed in a right angle to each other forming an L-shape. This house style is based on the then-popular Gothic Revival and corresponds to emerging new lifestyles of the time. One such example with a similar L-shape is the Red House, Morris' home designed by Philip Webb that Pevsner regarded as the origin of Modern residential architecture. The main wing features a hall and a corridor on the north side and various rooms arranged on the south side in order to provide these rooms with views on the grass-covered garden on south and over the cityscape and the river mouth beyond. The service staircase placed at the angle of the L-shape defines the boundary between the spaces for the master and the servants, while it serves as a point of focus of the building's exterior.

Small in size for a residence of this scale, the entrance is located on the western end of the building. Its external appearance is overly austere, but once inside, such impression is wiped out by a chain of exquisite spaces. The library which is the owner's study, the living room and the dining room are arranged along the line of flow on the north side that continues from the entrance, staircase and hall. Likewise, the upper floor has a corridor and a hall on the north side lined with several bedrooms, all of them skillfully decorated with differently-themed interior design.

The main spaces for the owner couple are given designs that are representative of the sense of gender of the time. While the library and the dining room are masculine spaces of

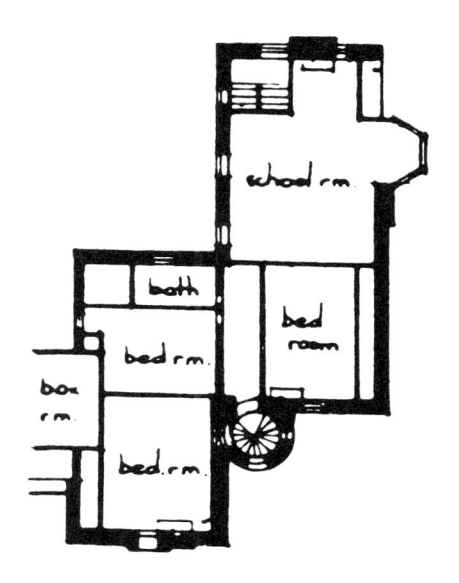

Second floor

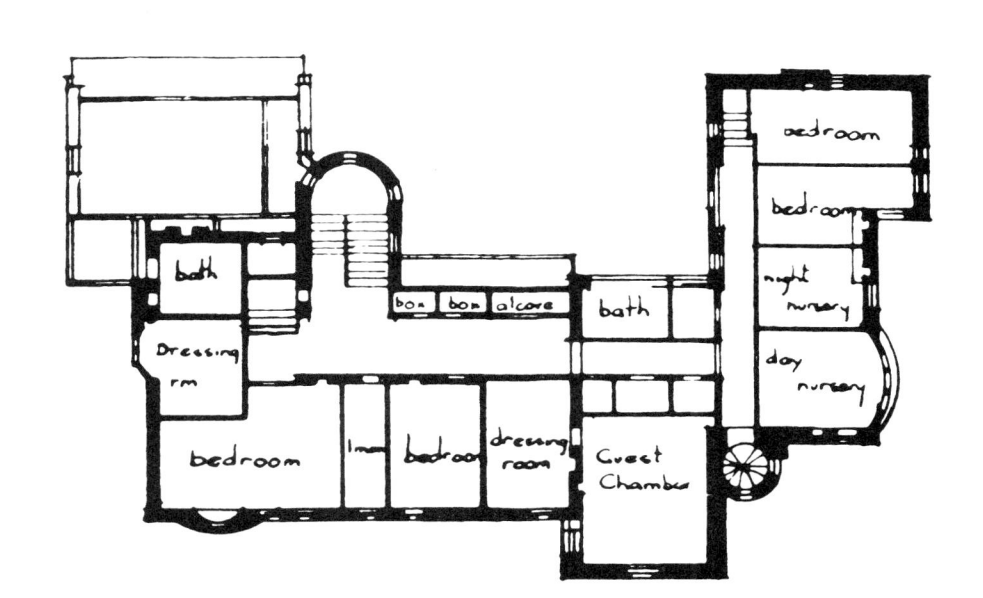

First floor

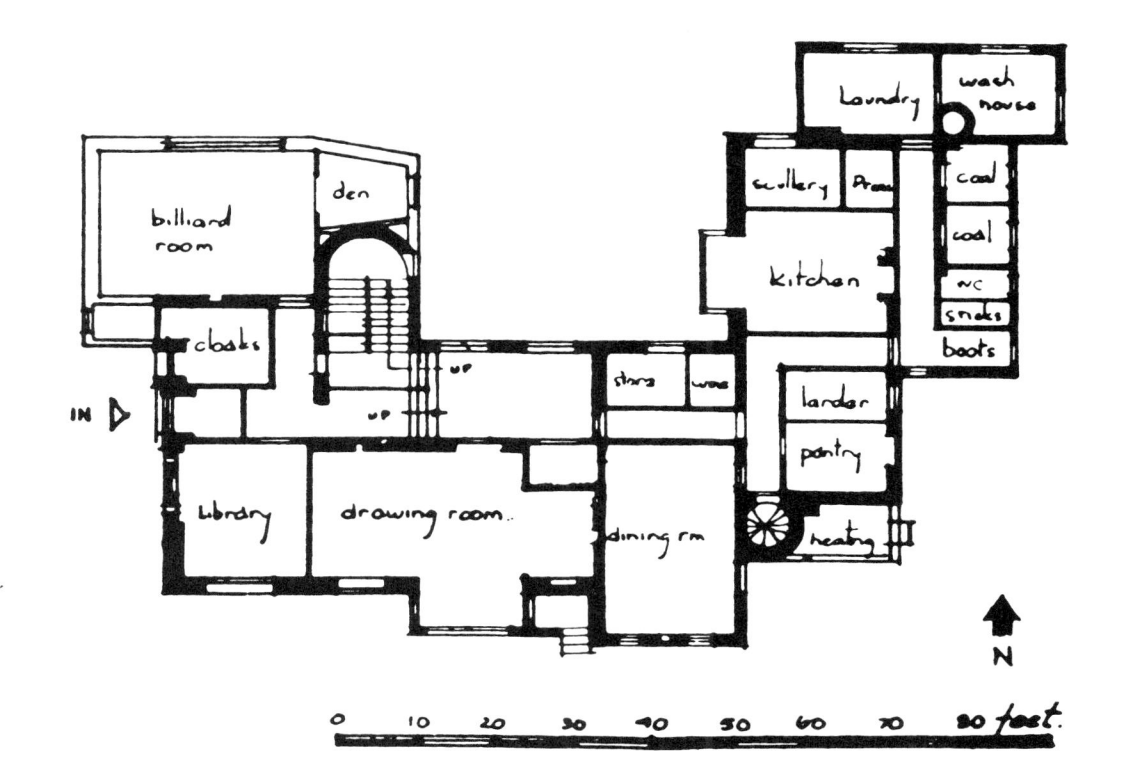

Ground floor

View toward Clyde River from hill

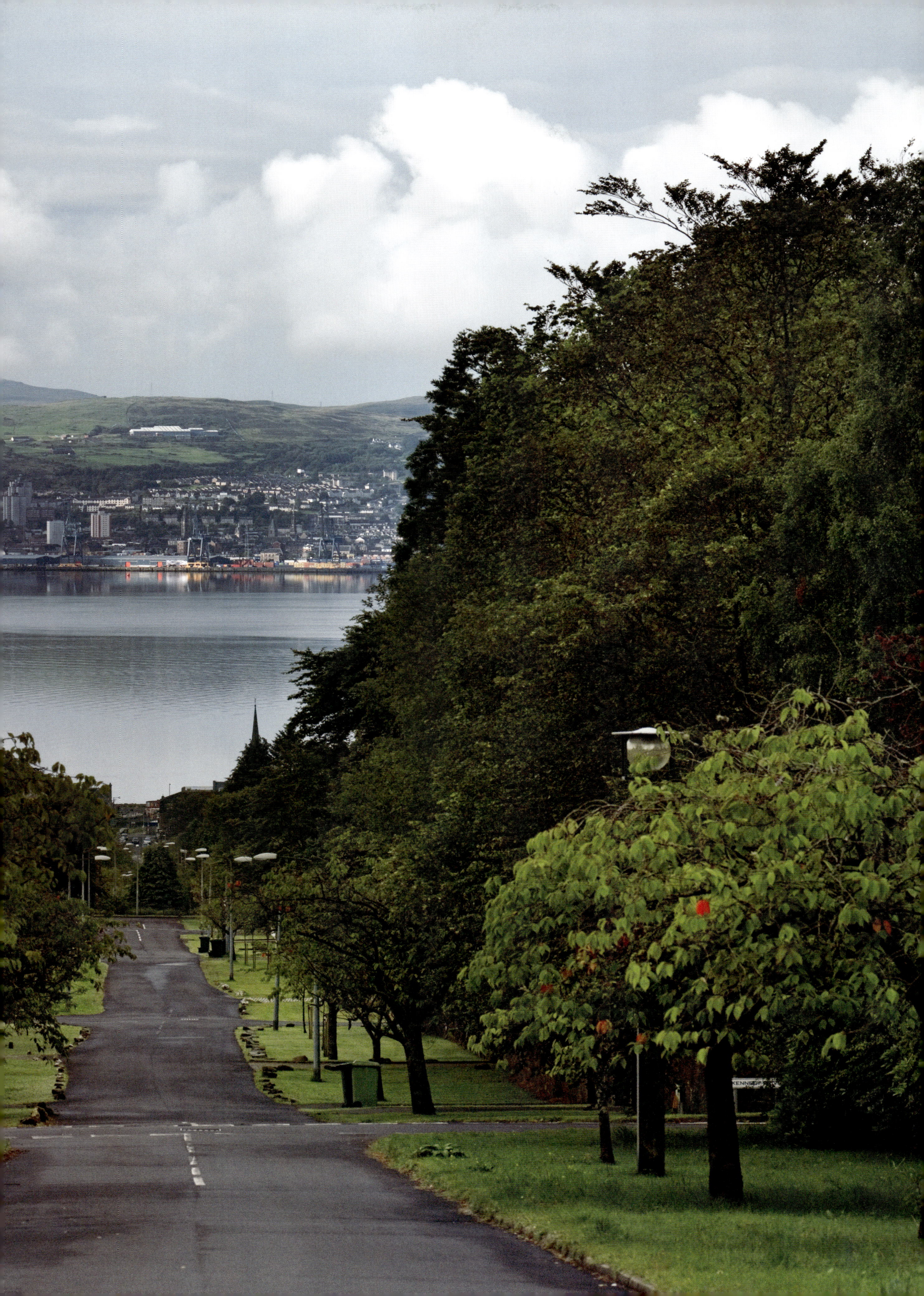

黒いステイン仕上げとされ，その素材感によって引き締められるフォーマルな性格の空間に仕立てられている。

　白を基調とした居間は明るい空間である。壁を彩る薔薇をモチーフにした曲線パターンと幾何学模様が繰り返し水平方向に連続する装飾は，どこか尾形光琳のグラフィカルな作品を思わせるジャポニズム調である。南側のアルコーブにはソファがつくり付けられ，大きく取られた窓は庭との距離感を縮めている。東側にもアルコーブが配置され，居間を変化のある空間にしている。

　2階主寝室は1階居間と同様，白の空間である。ここではさらに置かれた家具も白く塗られることでそれらの表情を抽象化し，より柔らかく清らかな女性的な空間に演出している。居間の壁面よりも具体的な絵柄の薔薇のパターンが白い壁面にちりばめられ，この部屋も夫人のものとして繊細な空間に仕立てられている。東側，一対の収納家具の扉には優雅なカーブと淡いピンクのポイントが与えられて，華やかに反対側のスリーピング・アルコーブと対面する。端正なデザインのベッドの置かれた西側のアルコーブはヴォールト天井により特別な場所として飾られる。

　2階ホールにもアルコーブが設けられている。ホールより2段のステップ分高い床を与えられ，一対のベンチが向き合うゴンドラの様なアルコーブは，2階ホールを単なる寝室群を結ぶ動線空間ではなく，前室的な空間に仕立てている。

　諸室を飾る豊富なディテール，その結果である内部空間の多様さにもかかわらず「ヒル・ハウス」が一つの「家」としてまとめあげられているという事実は，マッキントッシュが並外れたデザイン能力の持ち主であったことの証明に他ならない。そして，装飾は空間を重厚にしていくのが普通だが，「ヒル・ハウス」の装飾空間は近代・現代的な「軽さ」を纏っている。これはマッキントッシュがその天才的な感性をもって工芸と建築を見事なバランスで横断していたからである。後年オランダに現れるヘリット・リートフェルトが，家具職人と建築家の二つの職能を見事に使い分けて名作「シュローダー邸」で実現した空間の質と同等のものが「ヒル・ハウス」に展開している。

　ラッチェンスに見い出すことのできる建築家に求められる近代・現代性が，知性から大衆性までのマルチレイヤーに渡る総合的な操作の妙であるとするなら，マッキントッシュのそれは建築家の職能としてその後先鋭的に重要視されていく，類い稀なるデザイナーとしてのアーティスィックな能力と感性である。現代の建築家の使命の多様化，活動領域の拡張を予見する二タイプの現代建築家の出現であった。

'black' for the husband, the living room and the master bedroom on the upper floor are contrastingly feminine spaces of 'white.' Wooden details in the library and living room that are the men's spaces are finished with black stain whose firm and tight texture help create a space with a formal character.

　White-based living room is a bright space with walls decorated with curved, rose-motif pattern and continuous sequence of geometric horizontal pattern that are in the Japonisme style, somewhat reminiscent of Korin Ogata's graphical works. A sofa is built into the alcove on the south side, whose large window diminishes the sense of distance from the garden. Another alcove is set on the east side to add a varied touch to the living room.

　Master bedroom on upper floor is, as with the living room on ground floor, a space of white. Complete with furniture painted white as well, their expressions are abstracted and contribute in creating a softer and purer feminine space. White walls are covered with rose motifs that are more graphical than that on the living room walls to produce a delicate space for the lady. On the east side, a pair of storage furniture with doors featuring elegant curves and pale pink points stands gorgeously face to face with the sleeping alcove on the other side. The latter accommodates a bed in a clear-cut design and is decorated with a vaulted ceiling that gives the place a feeling of specialness.

　The upper-floor hall is also equipped with an alcove. With its floor two steps higher than the hall's and a pair of benches facing one another, this gondola-like alcove helps turn the upper-floor hall into an anteroom-like space and not a mere space for the line of flow that connects the bedrooms.

The fact that the Hill House is successfully put together as a 'home' in spite of the rich details adorning the rooms and the consequent diversity of internal spaces is nothing more or less than an evidence of Mackintosh's unique design ability. While it is usual for decorations to add a sense of gravity heaviness to the space, the decorative spaces in the Hill House is dressed up in a Modern/Contemporary 'lightness.' This was only possible because his gifted talents allowed Mackintosh to cross between crafts and architecture with a spectacular sense of balance. What can be seen in the Hill House is the same quality of space as that of the Schröder House, a masterpiece realized a few decades later by Gerrit Rietveld from the Netherlands as he successfully used both of his two professional abilities, as a furniture craftsman and an architect.

　If one of the Modern/Contemporary aspects required in an architect that can be found in Lutyens were to be the wizardry of his multi-layered, comprehensive manipulation that range from intelligence to popular appeal, the ones found in Mackintosh are his artistic competence and sensitivity as an exceptional designer that ultimately came to be radically viewed as professional abilities of much importance in later years. The emergence of these two types of Contemporary architects seemed to predict the coming of diversification of the Contemporary architect's mission and the expansion of his/her sphere of activity.

English translation by Lisa Tani

View from nothwest. Entrance on right

View from southwest. Entrance on left

Overall view from southeast

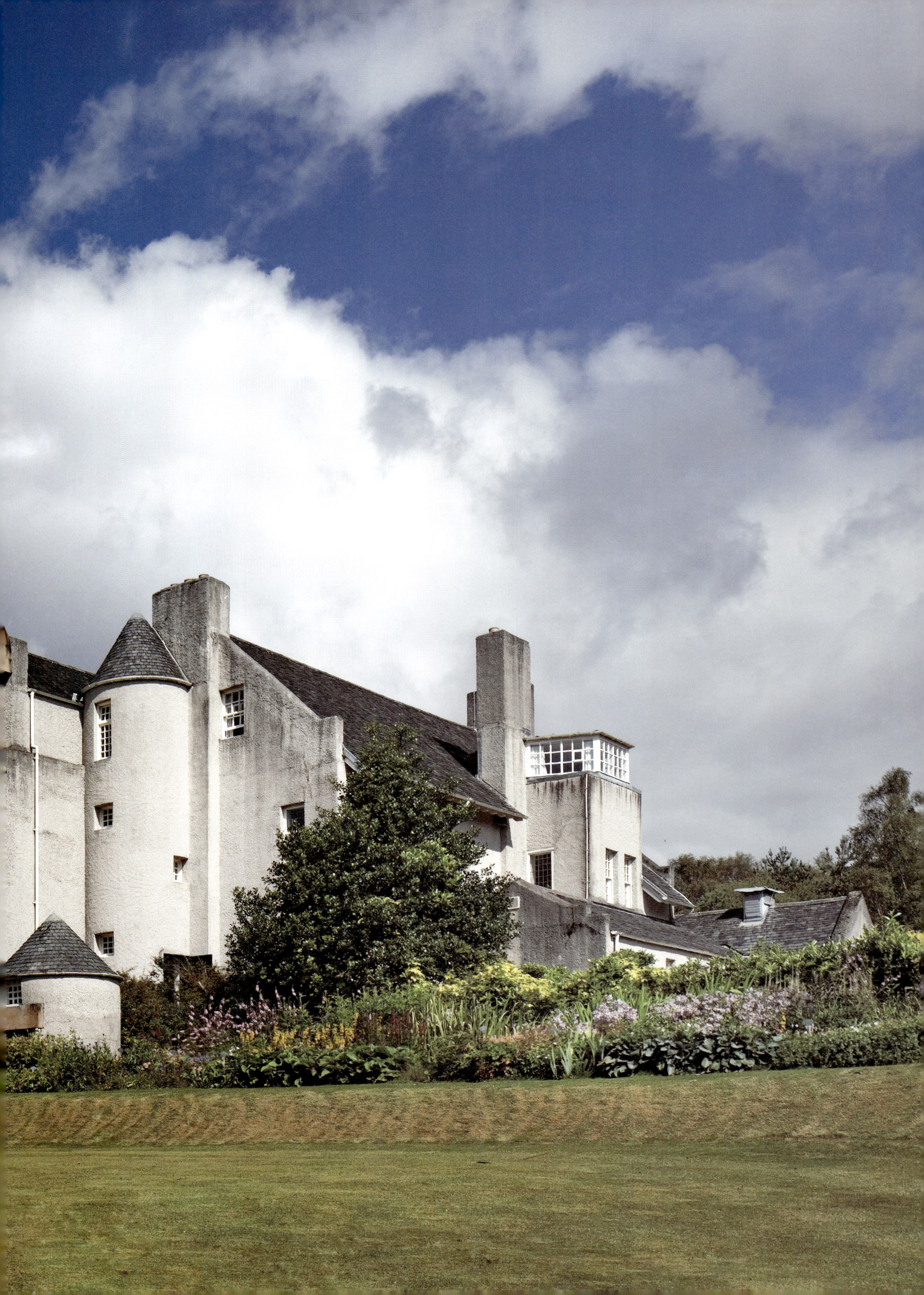

Wall detail of master bedroom

View from east

Courtyard on north

Main entrance on west

Courtyard on north: view of staircase

Hall: view from entrance

Hall: view toward entrance

Drawing room: view toward south

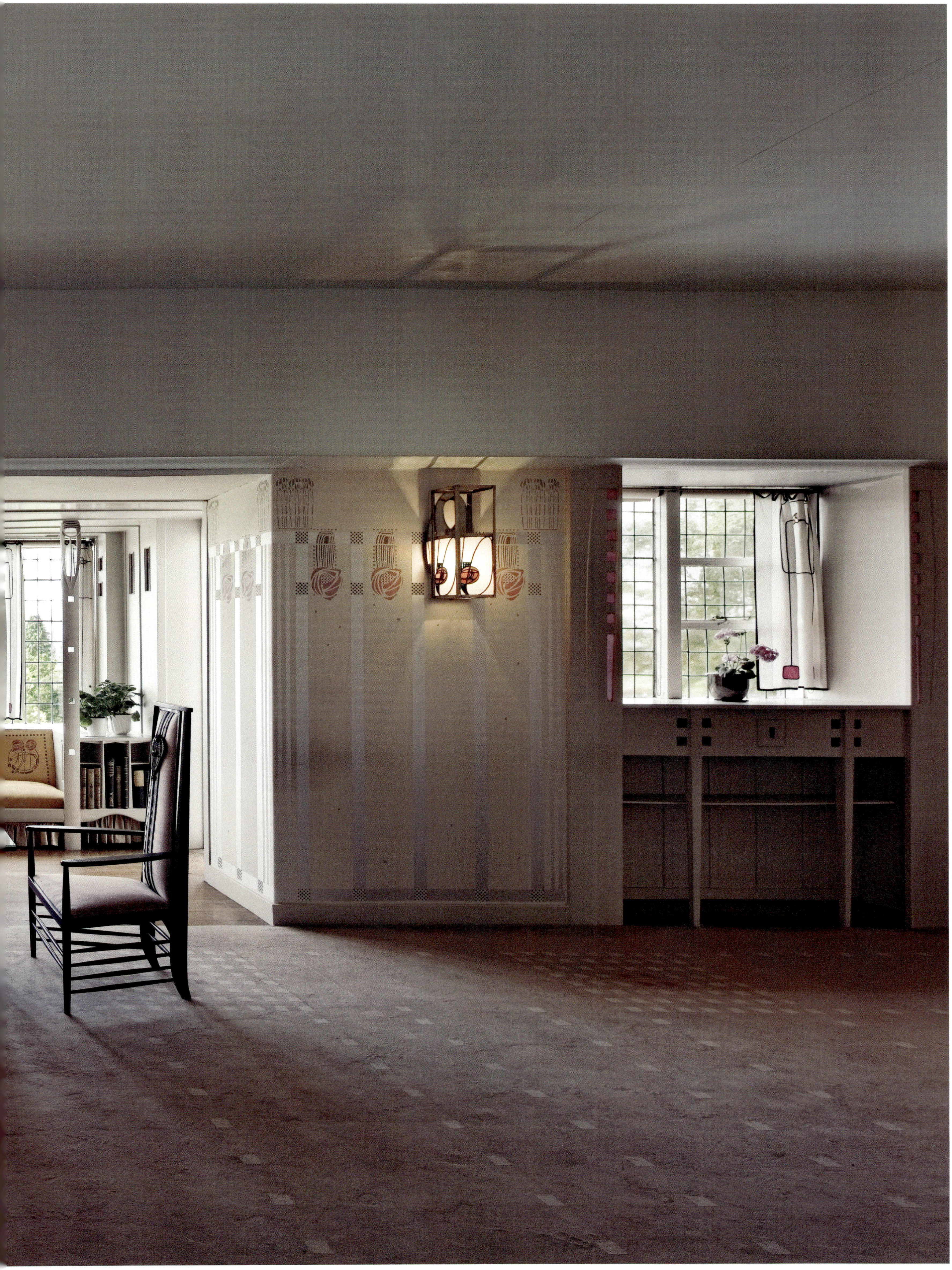

Drawing room: view toward east

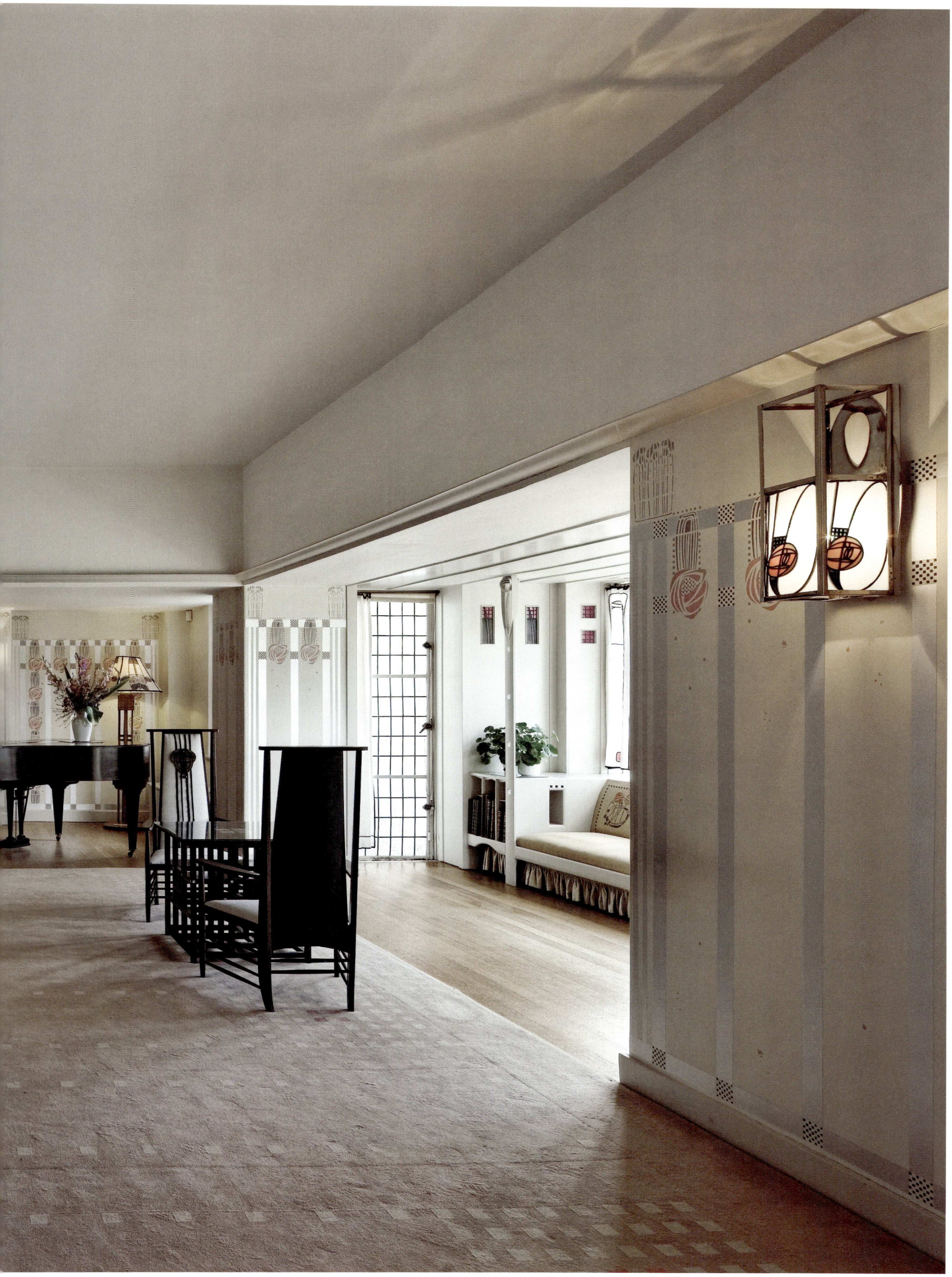

Drawing room: view toward west

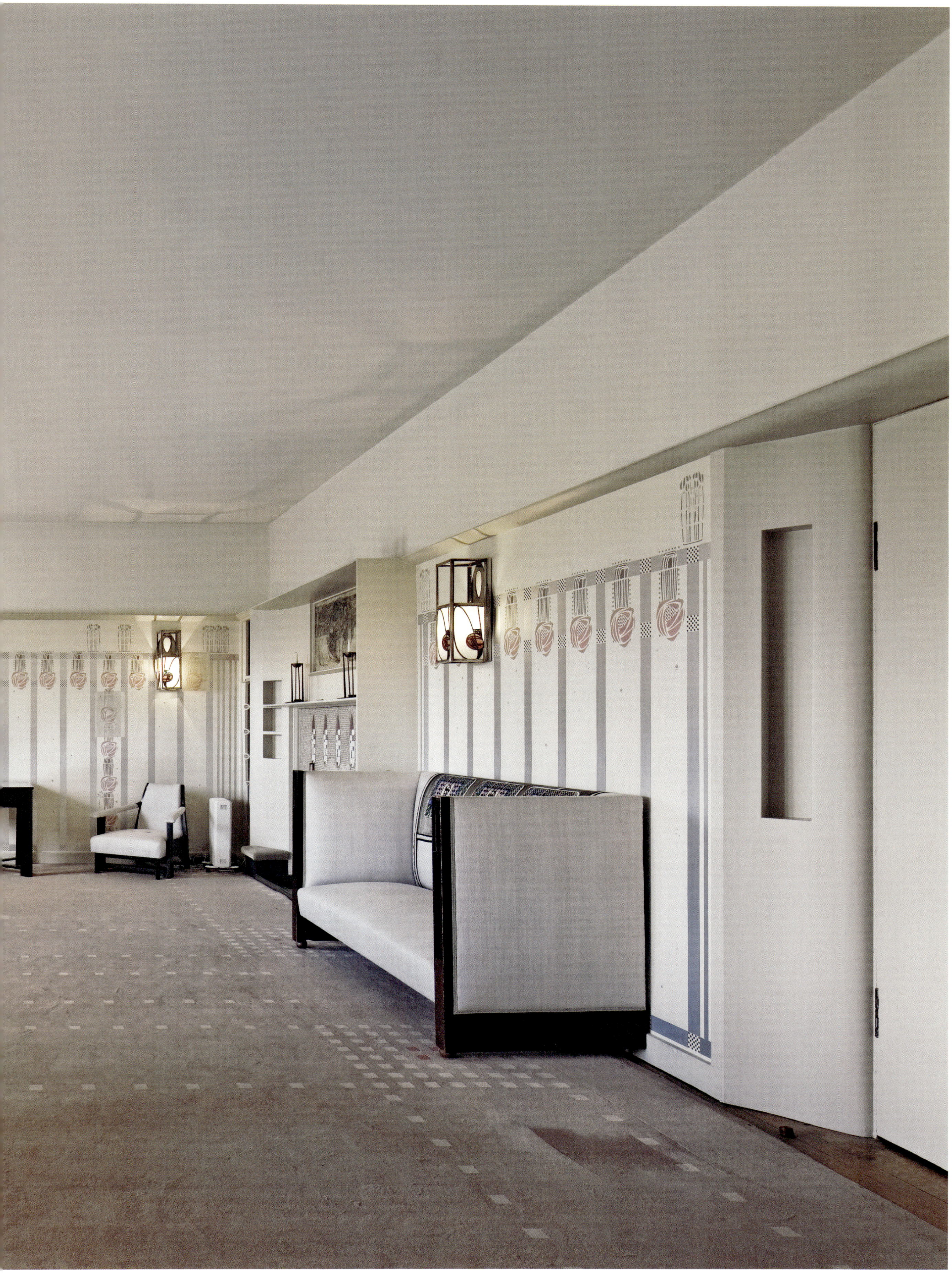

Northwest corner of drawing room

Alcove of drawing room

28

Fireplace of drawing room

Wall paper and light fixture of drawing room, designed by Architect

Furnishing of drawing room, designed by Architect

Table and chairs at drawing room, designed by Architect

Alcove for piano of drawing room

Alcove of drawing room

Dining room: view toward south

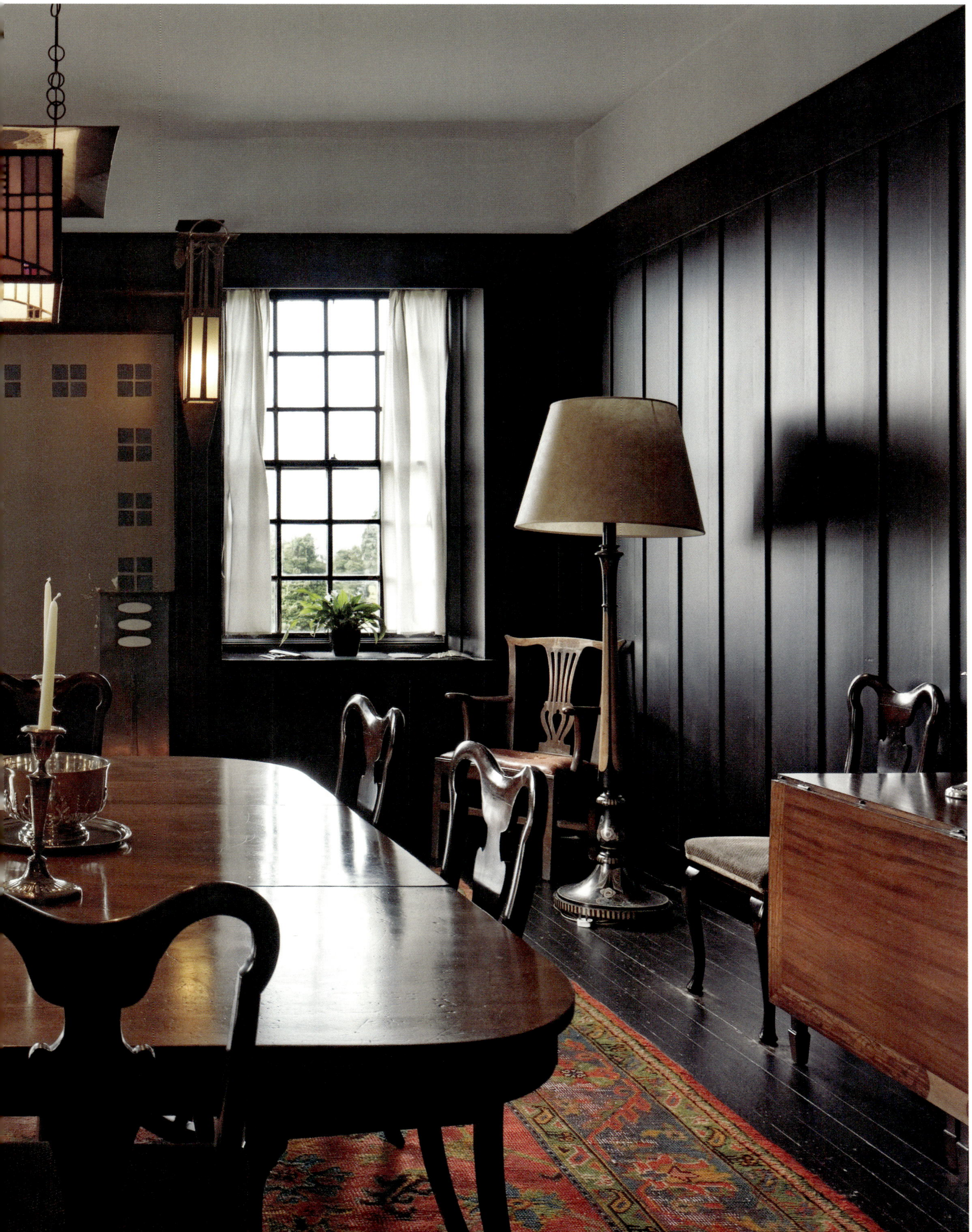

Dining room: view toward north

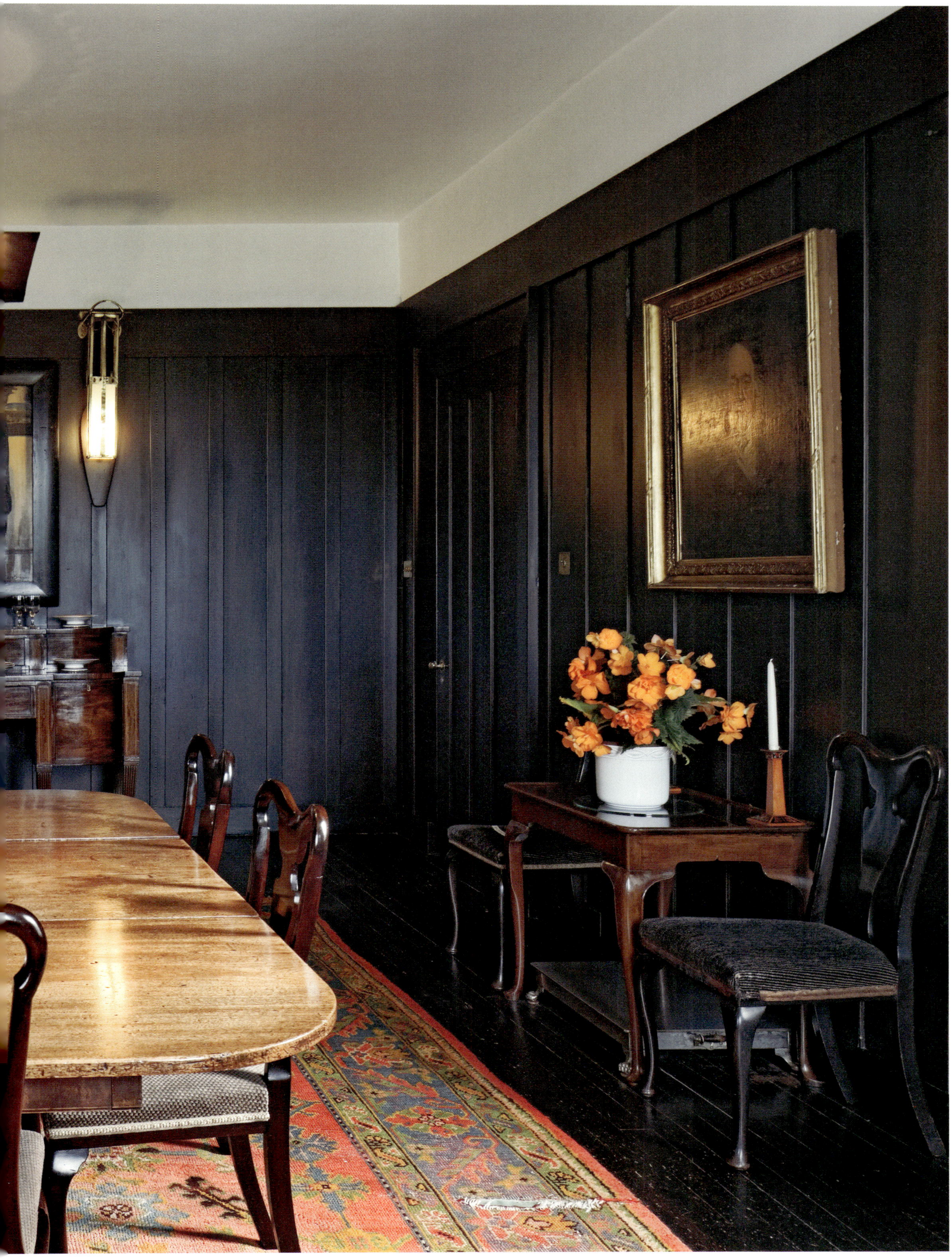

Fireplace of dining room

Light fixture of dining room

Light fixtures of hall

View from hall toward drawing room

Hall

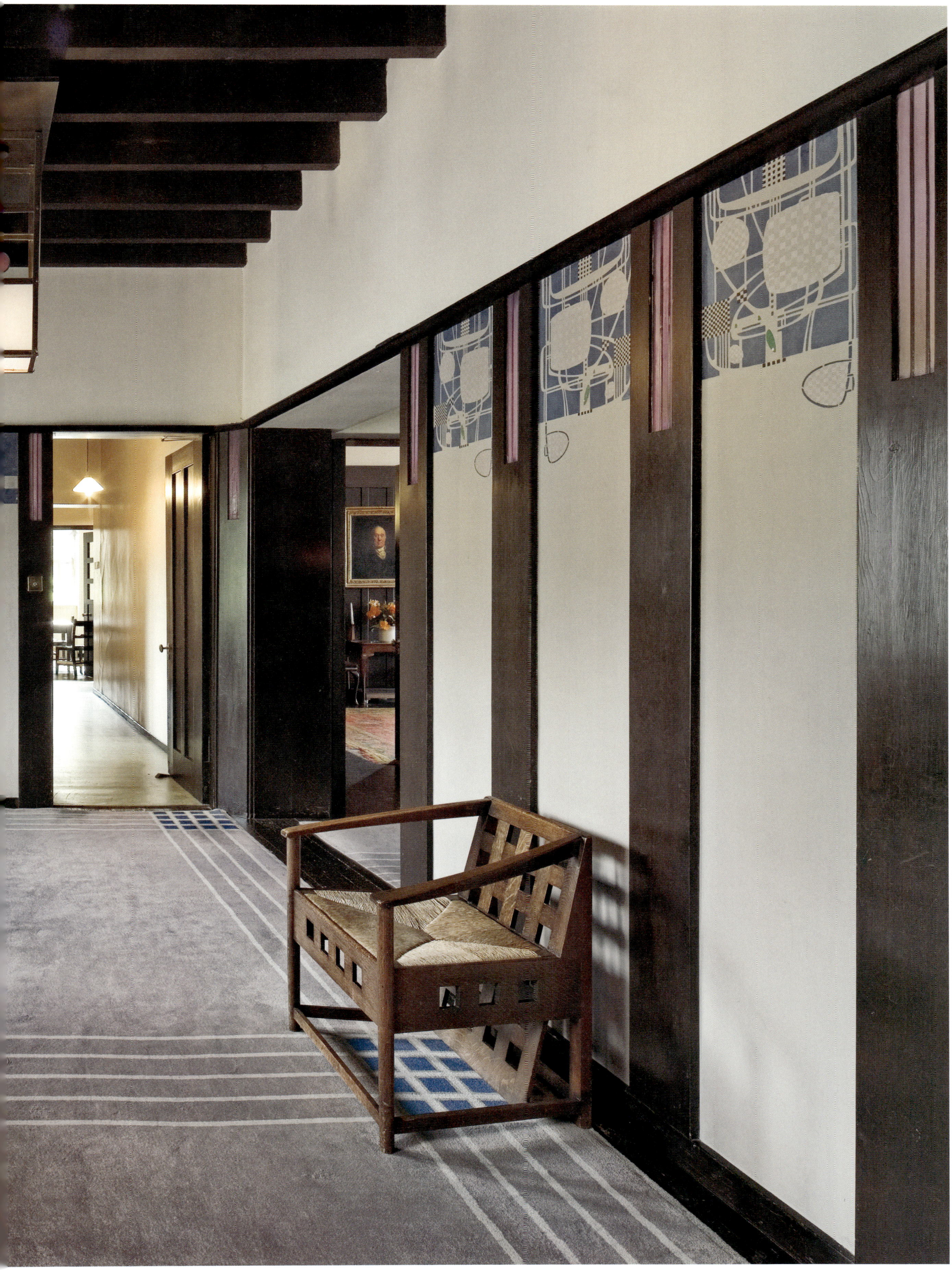

Hall: staircase to first floor on left

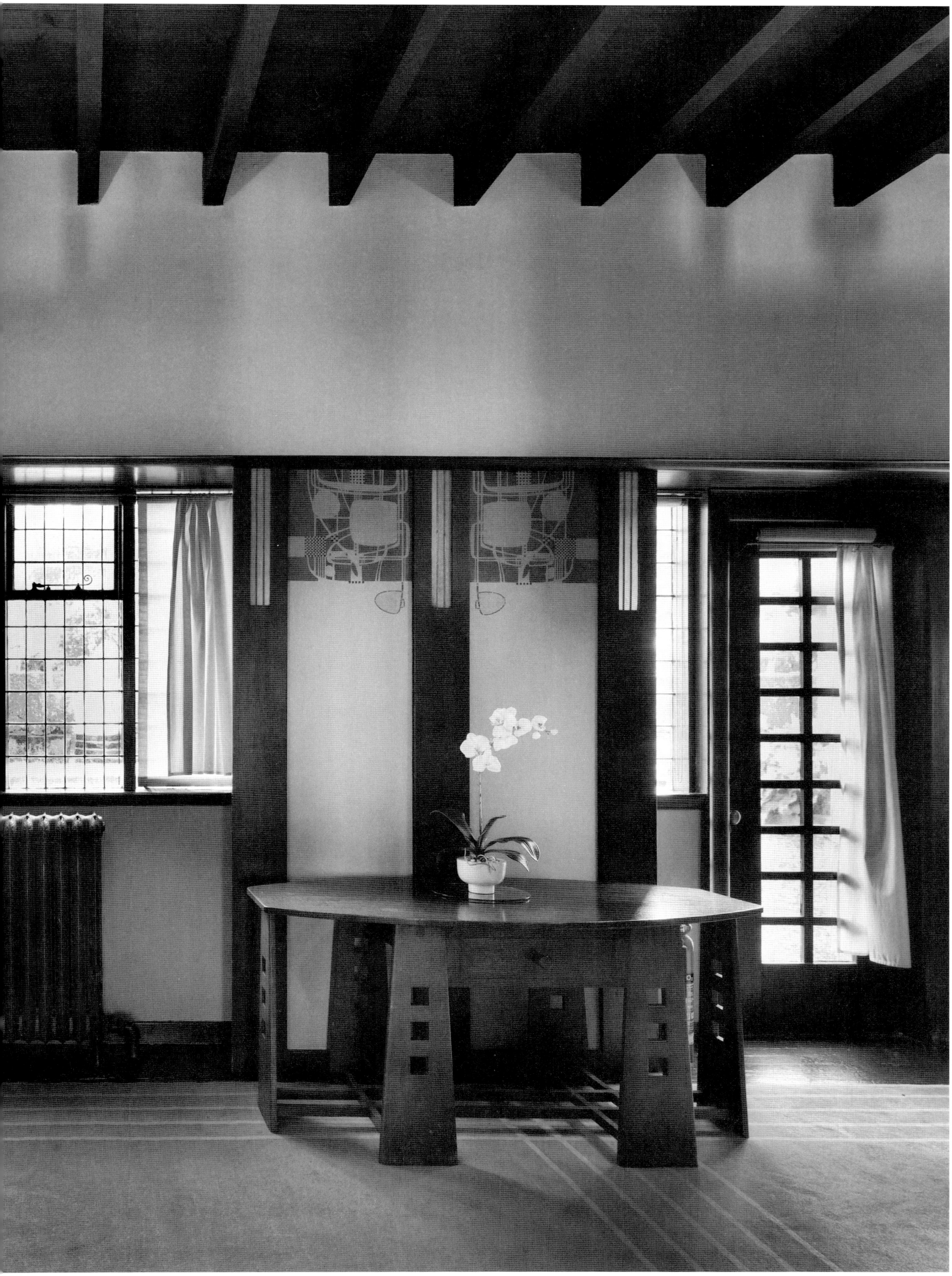

Library

Fireplace of library

Hall: entrance on left, staircase to first floor on right

Fireplace of hall

Light fixture of staircase

Staircase

Upper hall on first floor

Alcove of upper hall

Alcove of upper hall

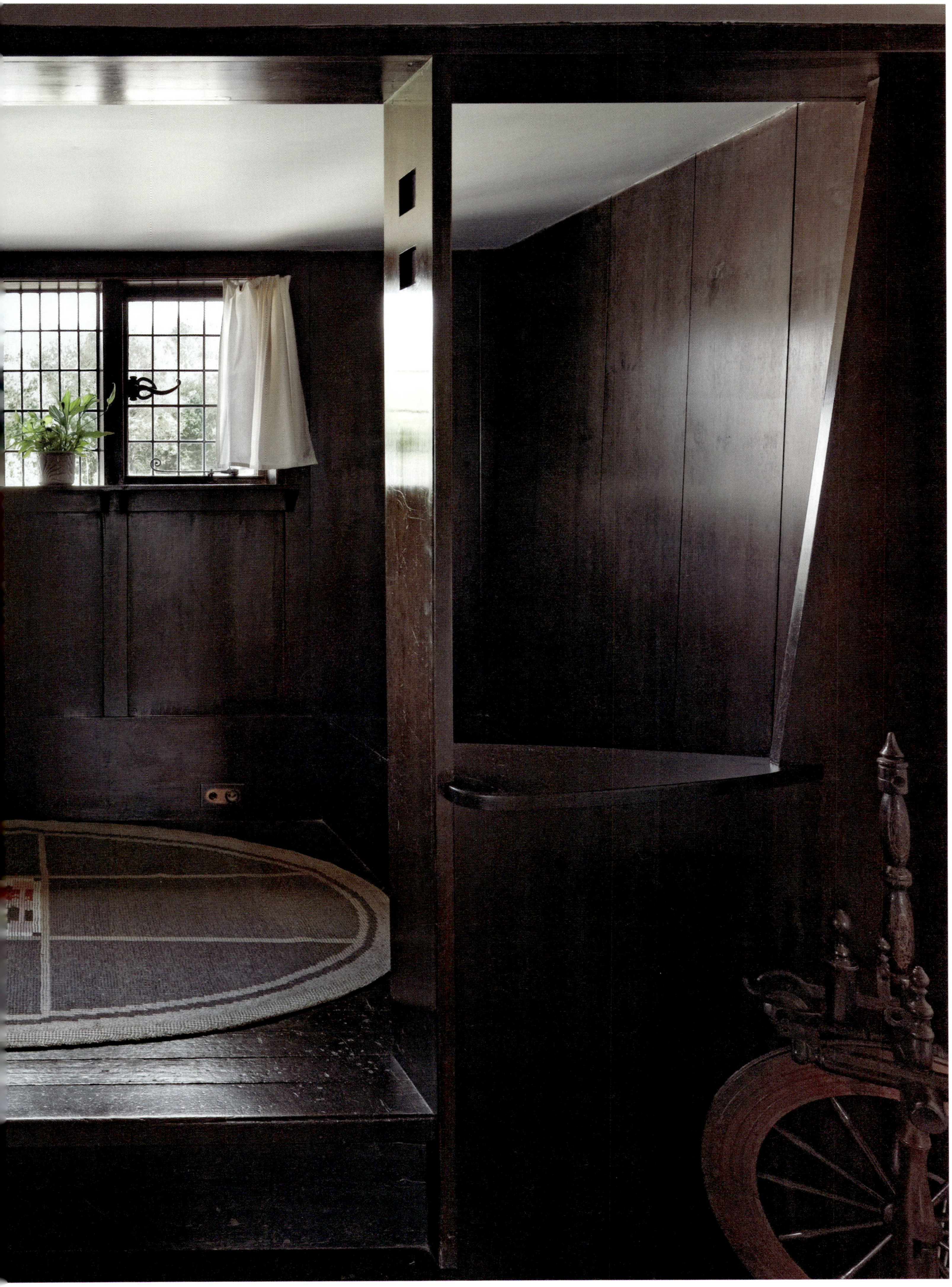

Master bedroom: view toward sleeping alcove

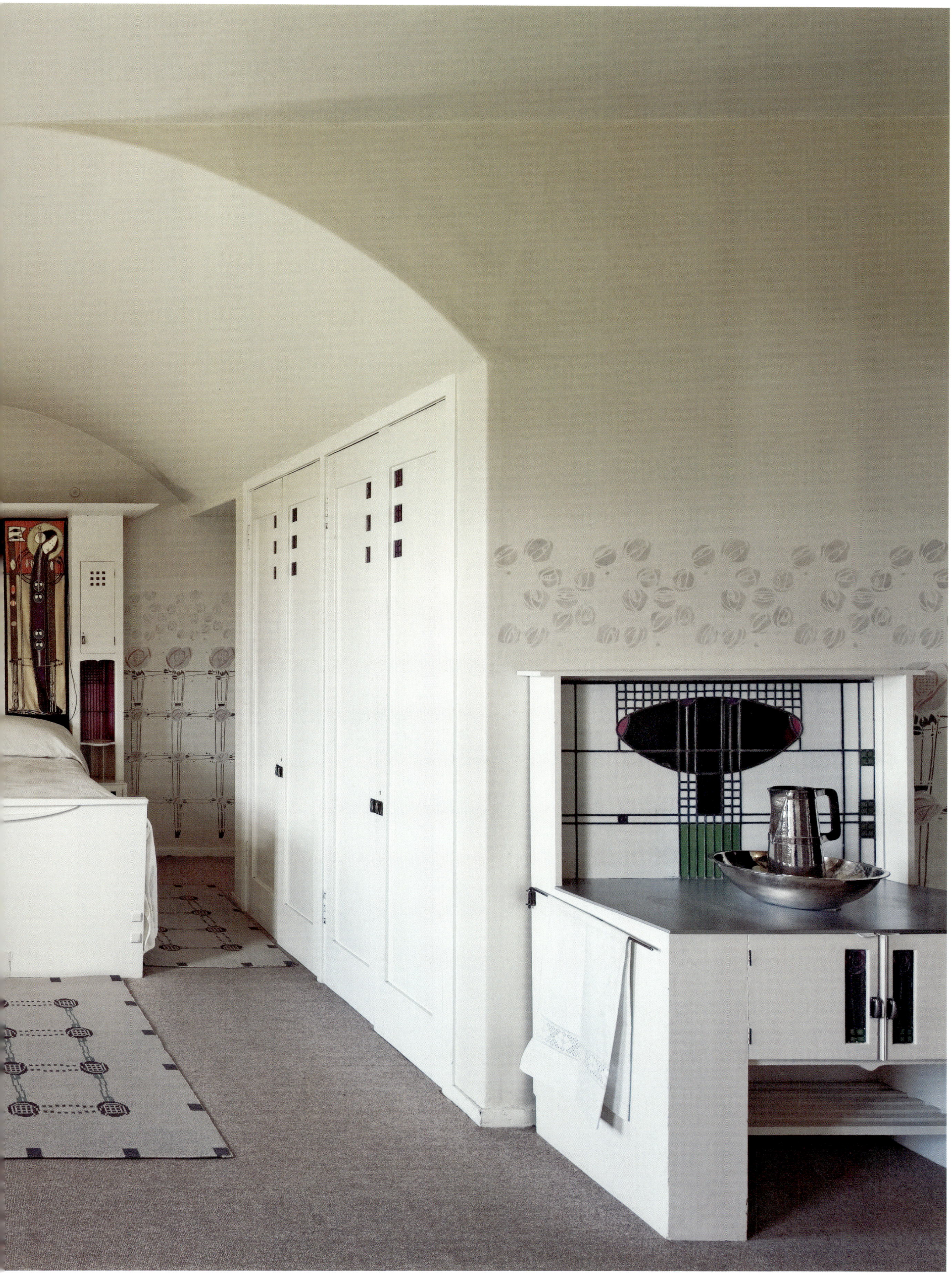

Master bedroom: view toward east

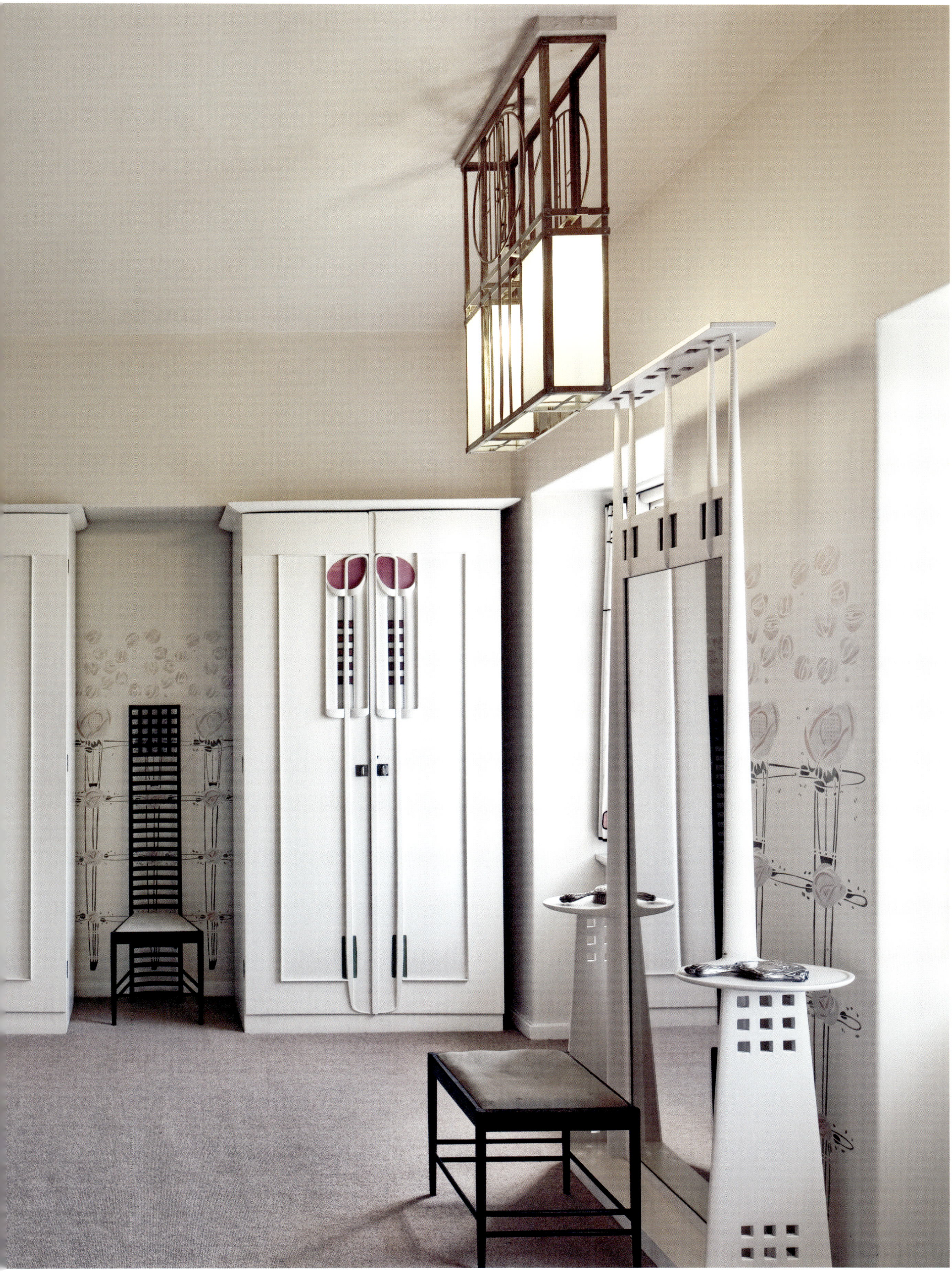

Master bedroom

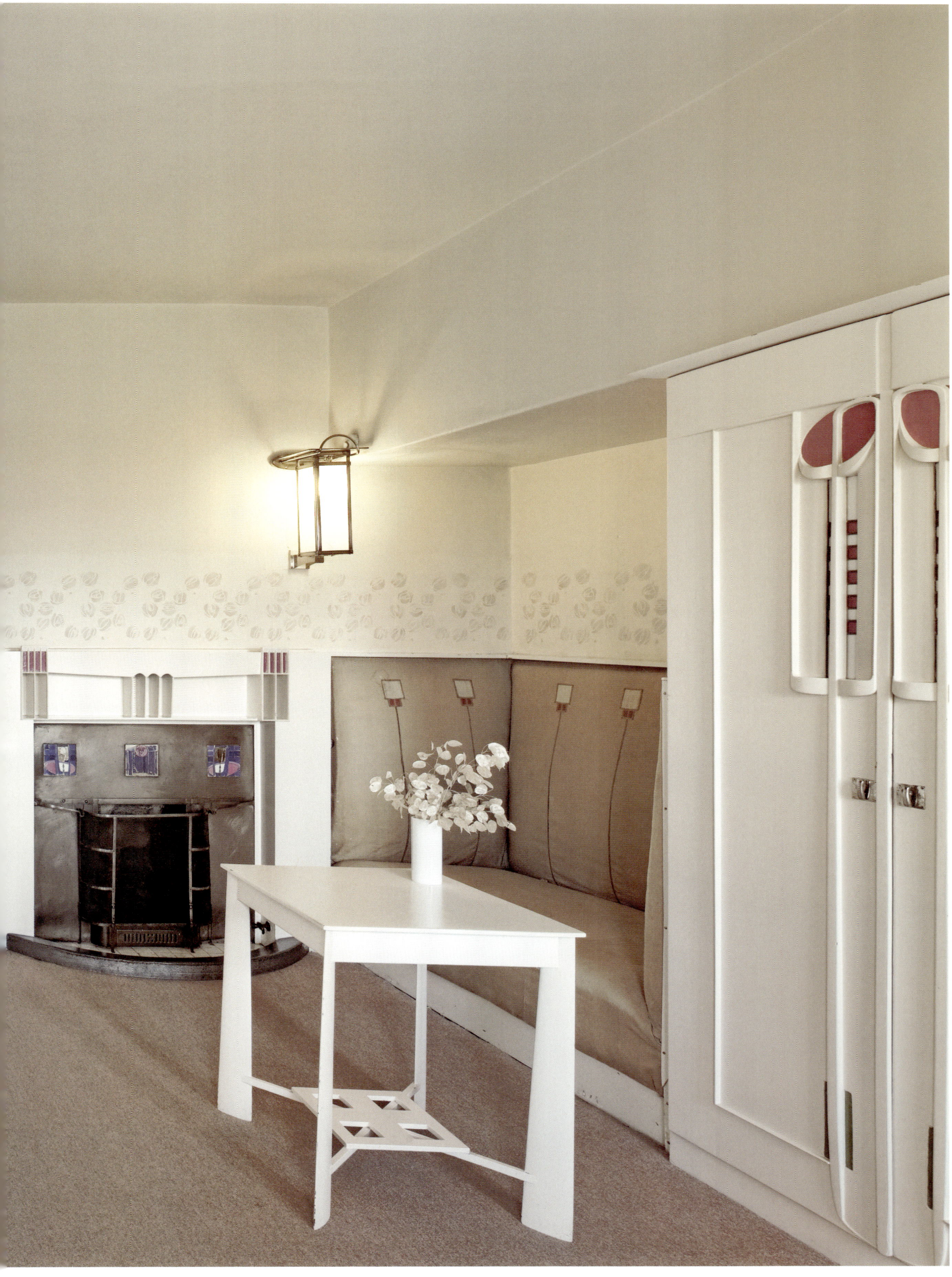

View from guest chamber toward Clyde River

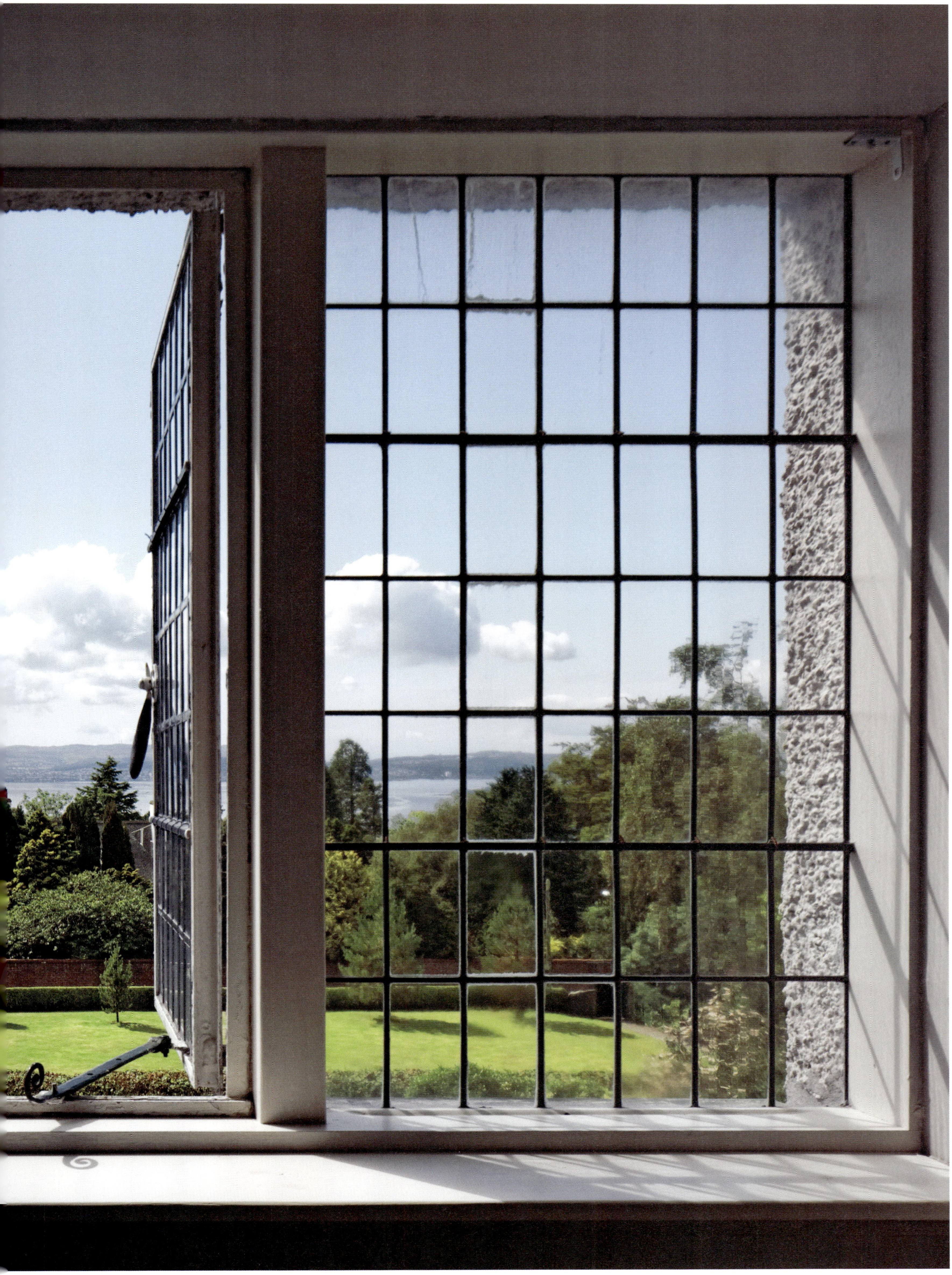

Acknowledgment of drawings:
"Mackintosh Architecture" (edited by Jackie Cooper and Barbara Bernard/Academy Editions, London, 1978)

世界現代住宅全集11
チャールズ・レニー・マッキントッシュ
ヒル・ハウス

2011年11月25日発行
文：二川由夫
企画・編集・撮影：二川幸夫
アート・ディレクション：細谷巖

印刷・製本：大日本印刷株式会社
制作・発行：エーディーエー・エディタ・トーキョー
151-0051　東京都渋谷区千駄ヶ谷3-12-14
TEL.(03)3403-1581(代)

禁無断転載
ISBN 978-4-87140-636-9 C1352